# Cosa Nostra News: The Cicale Files, Vol. 1 Inside the Last Great Mafia Empire

Dominick Cicale and Ed Scarpo

# DEDICATION

Dominick and I thank Robert Sberna of TheCrimeBeat.com and Mattie for their tireless efforts in making this a better book.

I thank Dominick Cicale, who survived incredible circumstances unimaginable to most of us. He turned his life around and I am proud to call him my friend.

And to the readers of Cosa Nostra News blog, without whom this book never would have happened.

# CONTENTS

# INTRODUCTION
## BY ED SCARPO

This is not a biography. Rather, it is the first of an intended series of books about the Mafia based on Dominick Cicale's experiences. A former capo in the Bonanno crime family, Dominick befriended and associated with numerous high-ranking figures within all five of New York's crime families (Gambino, Genovese, Luchese and Colombo are the other four).

Born and raised in the Bronx, New York, Cicale initially had ties to the Genovese crime family, but after serving a prison stint and meeting capo Anthony "Bruno" Indelicato, he changed course and headed for the Bonanno family in 1999. He forged a tight alliance with Vincent "Vinny Gorgeous" Basciano, then an up-and-coming member of the Bronx faction.

In January 2006, the bond between Cicale and Basciano ended. In this installment, we concentrate on Dominick's experience and insight into Joseph Massino's last years in power. Massino is often referred to as the Last Don (hence, this book's title). We view through a powerful lens the brutal murder of Gerlando "George from Canada" Sciascia and its resulting impact on the relations between the Bonanno family in New York and its "Canadian wing" in Montreal established by the Mafia Commission in 1931 and formalized by Carmine Galante in the 1950s.

Volume One's cast of characters further includes high-ranking Bonanno Mafiosi such as Salvatore "Sal the Iron Worker" Montagna, Michael "Mikey Nose" Mancuso—and of course Cicale and his former mentor, Vinny Gorgeous (who was never referred to by that nickname in person).

My initial choice for this book's title was "A Bronx Tale," but obviously it's been used. And this is no tale—this is factual, backed by research I conducted to set the stage for Dominick, who testified in four major racketeering trials and served a 10-year sentence. (A full bibliography is included at the end.) Like Cicale, many key figures in this book lived in the Bronx, "an entity unto itself," says Cicale. Bonanno family members based outside the Bronx rarely venture there if they can help it, he says. "It's considered a backwater among many of the Brooklyn, Queens and Manhattan guys." However, Cicale adds, "the Bronx neighborhoods are still strong and until this day I am the only high-profile rat who came out of the Bronx."

# 1 THE BADGE

On a summer night in 2003, Vincent "Vinny Gorgeous" Basciano and Dominick Cicale drove along the FDR Drive, departing Manhattan and heading toward the Bronx where both lived. A few weeks earlier Cicale had been formally inducted into the Bonanno crime family, with Basciano acting as his mentor.

Cicale skillfully navigated his Mercedes-Benz CL500 along the congested highway while the two listened to the sports radio chatter of 1010 WINS.

Vinny reached for the radio to lower the volume, then looked at Dominick. "Bo," he said, using a mob term that denotes respect, "do you feel any different now?"

Dominick glanced at Vinny and quickly replied. "Are you kidding? Why should I feel different just because I'm a made man? It's all bullshit; you know that. Only a punk would feel different and start walking around with his chest puffed out thinking he's somebody special. No, I don't feel different. I am still Dominick, take it or leave it."

Today, more than a decade after that conversation, Cicale says he is still "just Dominick." Seven years ago, Cicale turned government informant. But he says neither his status as a made man or a mob turncoat has ever caused him to change his principles. "I might be considered a rat now, but I will never run," he says. Cicale, who refused to enter the Federal Witness Protection Program, vows, "If someone tries to cross a line, to do harm to me or my family, all bets are off."

Not that he's particularly worried about mob retribution. "In my experience in organized crime, it seemed that about 85 percent of the made men in the streets were fucking punks who hid behind their badges [a mob term for button]. It's a joke," he says. At the same time, he doesn't live in a false comfort zone. One of these made men is quite capable of putting a bullet or two in his head, Cicale well knows.

Dominick expresses disdain for mob guys who publicly celebrate their induction. In his view, celebrating such a secret and illegal act (it is against federal law to belong to an organized crime group) is absurd. Off the radar is where mob guys belong.

"The Feds didn't even discover that I was a made guy until I became a capo and my big-mouth best friend Vinny Basciano bragged to an informant," says Dominick, adding that Vinny should have known that the informant was wearing a wire. "If Vinny hadn't talked, the Feds never would've even known about me."

Ironically, Cicale had always regarded Basciano as cautious and tight-lipped. In fact, Basciano's discretion was noted by Anthony DeStefano, in his book, Vinny Gorgeous: The Ugly Rise and Fall of a New York Mobster. DeStefano reported that while Cicale and Basciano were at lawyer Tommy Lee's office to hear recordings made by ex-Bonanno capo James "Big Lou" Tartaglione—the tapes were released as part of trial preparation— "Basciano didn't like the way he sounded... because [he had] said too much— particularly for a man who supposedly didn't do anything... It disturbed Cicale more that Basciano had seemed almost flip about him when talking to Tartaglione, a man long suspected of being an informant."

According to Cicale, Basciano took credit on the tapes for helping him, Cicale, evolve from a hoodlum into a businessman. (Doing the reverse— turning a businessman into a hoodlum—was impossible, Basciano also had noted.) Cicale next heard Basciano confide to Tartaglione that Dominick was his acting capo. Basciano's naïveté stunned Cicale. Basciano apologized, "but the damage had been done," as DeStefano noted. "Thanks to Basciano, he had become a person of interest to the feds."

"I couldn't fucking believe it," Dominick says now. "Vinny's talking to a guy that he knew might be wearing a wire—and what does he do? He mentions me by my name and then starts bragging about a murder. I was the New York Mafia's last best secret."

Dominick Cicale is still unsettled by conversations about his arrest and decision to become a government cooperator. Cicale is generally a soft-spoken, thoughtful man; he only reveals his hard-edged gangster past when these subjects are broached. Ten years ago, Cicale had been completely off the Fed's radar; the FBI did not know a Mafia member named Dominick Cicale existed, even following his promotion to capo. To illustrate how successful Cicale was at staying off the Fed's radar screen, consider Al D'Arco, a former Luchese acting boss who also turned state's evidence. While D'Arco was so secretive that only one surveillance photo of him exists, Cicale was even more successful: He was never captured on a single frame of film or in a photograph and his voice was never recorded on a wiretap.

Basciano also maintained a relatively low profile for most of his criminal career. According to Cicale, Basciano only began strutting around like a John Gotti-style mobster in expensive suits and brightly colored silk neckties ("showboating," says Cicale) after he became acting boss of the Bonanno family and the power went to his head. Earlier, for most of the years they were on the street together, Dominick and Vinny dressed down, donning jeans and baseball caps in daytime. The two dressed up only for evening social occasions. If they went out together, Cicale and Basciano usually were accompanied by their women.

Cicale and Vinny talked every day while on the street, always changing their routine, meeting at different times and places—sometimes in cemeteries late at night. These meetings continued even when Basciano anointed himself acting boss of the Bonanno crime family after Joseph Massino was locked up.

For outsiders, it may be difficult to understand the tight-knit relationship that Cicale and Basciano once had. Such a close allegiance is rare among Mafiosi, many of whom will never speak their heart to another member. The two men were so close that they once made a blood pact: If Bonanno crime family boss Joe Massino ever decreed one of their deaths, Cicale and Basciano would take Massino out—or die trying.

"Vinny was one of the ballsiest Mafiosi in New York during his last couple of decades on the streets," recalled Cicale. "Even though he had a glass jaw, he fought at the drop of a dime. Sometimes he'd get his ass kicked—but he didn't care. He was a stone-cold killer—so he'd retaliate by whacking the other guy."

Dominick, about eight years younger than Basciano, remains well-muscled and still has a mobster's dead-eyed stare. During his years on the street, he had a reputation as a competent and fearless fighter, a rarity among wiseguys. Before and after his induction, Dominick was always willing to brawl to defend himself or his friends, even if his combatant was a made man. "C'mon, let's take our badges off and settle this," he'd say. No one ever accepted his offer.

Vinny and Dominick were not only legitimate tough guys, but also huge earners. However, the cautious Massino didn't know what to make of Basciano; the Last Don was so wary of him that he avoided the man for years. Massino had heard stories about Basciano brawling and even killing people "off the record," which in Mafia parlance means "acts committed against the rules, but kept secret." Over time, however, Massino reconsidered the young mobster, appreciating that he was loyal and generous with his tributes. Massino also recognized that Vinny was a natural-born leader.

When Basciano took control of the family after Massino's 2003 incarceration, the jailed mob boss respected and supported the Bronx capo's ballsy move. Assuming the reigns of a crime family in such tumultuous times, when the FBI was flipping made men left and right, required utter fearlessness. Few members even wanted to step up; Vinny Basciano didn't have to think twice.

Richard "Shellackhead" Canterella once recalled Massino telling him, "If anything happened to me [Massino], Vinny will hold the family together."

"The only thing is that Vinny has got to slow down; he's too quick," Massino added, holding his forefinger and thumb in the shape of a gun.

Massino, while imprisoned, held his tongue as Basciano implemented changes in personnel. One exception involved Sal "The Iron Worker" Montagna, whom Massino slated for demotion. Vinny disagreed with the call, according to Cicale, and simply ignored the order. Massino either never found out or didn't bother to relay his response to his acting boss.

"Joe was not coming home anytime soon and this was Vinny's show," said Cicale, who further noted he believed Vinny exceeded his authority while serving as acting boss. "The power went to his head," said Cicale, who nevertheless remained not only an enthusiastic Basciano supporter—but also Vinny's chief enforcer.

When Vinny began ordering men to strip at meetings, including induction ceremonies, the Mafia's most solemn occasion, some mobsters voiced annoyance. Cicale, however, agreed with Basciano, believing desperate times call for desperate measures. Dominick's loyalty to Vinny was so absolute that Basciano thought nothing of ordering him to break a cardinal rule of the American Mafia, or Cosa Nostra (Our Thing, in Italian). Basciano instructed Dominick to "put his hands on" a made member of the crime family—meaning he told Dom to administer a beating.

"That was a big no-no," Cicale said. "But Vinny didn't give a shit, so I did what I was told. In my eyes, Vinny was always my boss. I never liked or cared for Joe Massino. I always felt that he was a piece of shit. This was based on nothing more than a gut feeling. I was there for one person—Vincent Basciano."

The man targeted by Basciano for punishment was Gino Gillespie.

"Gino was being disrespectful," Cicale said. "Gino sometimes failed to show up at meetings; sometimes he'd arrive 30 minutes late. Basciano was tired of Gino's defiance and decided to send a message so that everyone in the crime family knew who was in charge. Gino lived on Staten Island and knew we couldn't monitor him properly. He thought he was slick, figuring that we would get fed up with him and 'shelve' him. That's actually what Gino wanted. Then he'd be free to run around doing whatever he wanted."

In the Mafia, shelving someone means removing all the rights and privileges to which a made member is entitled; they aren't even allowed to earn. It's basically an option to getting rid of someone other than murdering him, typically because the person egregiously broke Mafia rules. To be shelved was considered disgraceful. These days, however, Dominick says

4

some members feeling the heat either from law enforcement or the mob may actually want to be shelved so they can disappear. To old-school Mafiosi, however, the notion of *wanting* to get shelved is unthinkable.

With Gino, Cicale recalled, "We had two options: give him what he wanted and shelve him—or we could kill him. Vinny considered both options, then ordered me to surprise Gino at his attorney's office. We knew he'd be there to attend a co-defendants' meeting. There I'd be able to find out what was on his mind. I was also given the order to fuck him up if he showed any disrespect toward me."

Dominick was not unconcerned about this particular assignment, as he knew it could—technically speaking—get him killed if Massino, who at the time was still very much the official boss, found out. Then again, Massino was occupying a jail cell. Acting boss Vinny Basciano ran the street for the Bonanno family. And Cicale had already bet all his chips on Vinny; he did whatever the boss asked.

Dominick, accompanied by "Louie Electric," drove to Gino's attorney's office. The two gangsters entered the building and waited in the hallway outside the lawyer's office near the men's room. Eventually, a Bonanno family member showed up to use the restroom, and Cicale and his partner confronted him.

"Go get Gino and tell him to go into the restroom," Cicale told the Bonanno soldier.

Louie Electric pulled a piece of paper from his pocket, unfolded it and stuck it to the door of the men's room using a wad of chewing gum from his mouth. The improvised notice read: "Out of Order." The two went inside. Soon enough, the door creaked open and Gino walked in, looking slightly shaken—perhaps from the sign on the door. He quickly regained his composure.

"Gino, what's up?" Dominick asked.

Gino stood his ground, arms folded, silently staring back at Dominick through a pair of tinted eyeglasses. "Gino was looking at me like he was some kind of king and I was a peasant," Cicale said.

So Dominick started with a verbal lashing. "Who the fuck do you think you are? You leave me waiting on street corners and you never show up. Or you show up an hour late. Who the fuck are you to make me wait?"

Gino's continued silent defiance was his only response. Dominick slowly walked toward Gino and before the Bonanno soldier comprehended what was happening, Cicale threw a left-right combo—a snapping uppercut, followed by a solid right—at his face. Gino crumpled to the floor, his head landing in the bottom of one of the urinals. When Gino was pulled back on his feet, his defiance was sapped. All he had to show for it were a swollen darkening eye, loose tooth and gashed, bloody lip. His hair was matted down on one side of his head from urinal water.

"Yes, this came from above," Dominick said. "I strongly advise you to start showing respect. If I want to meet with you at 3 a.m. in the morning, you better be there. Or next time might be your last time. Got it?"

Gino, holding what was left of his eyeglasses, apologized and confirmed his loyalty. He'd be the most punctual member of the Bonanno family from now on, he promised. Gino was now "in check," as Cicale called it.

"I had his undivided attention for the rest of our involvement," said Dominick. "Vinny did not play games. The worst thing a guy could do to Vinny was show disrespect. If someone was disrespectful, they'd face severe consequences. Neither of us were showboats who just talked a good game. We handled whatever needed handling—and then we'd deal with whatever consequences followed. We didn't need any bullshit badge to make us men."

# 2  MASSINO'S LAST MURDER

In March 1999, Salvatore "Good Lookin' Sal" Vitale celebrated his nephew's silver wedding anniversary at Amici restaurant on Long Island. A gathering of family and friends participated in the lively festivities.

Among the invited was Joseph "Big Joey" Massino, all 300 pounds of him. He arrived late. It was a happy occasion but Massino's mind was on serious mob business. Massino pulled aside Vitale, who was his brother-in-law (Massino married Vitale's sister) as well as his underboss.

The two huddled by themselves at the end of one of the long tables and Massino whispered to Sal: "George has got to go."

Massino, boss of the Bonanno crime family, one of the storied Five Families of New York, had just ordered Vitale to murder one of their own—a respected, longtime member of the family who had taken up arms to defend Massino's right to the top position.

Gerlando "George from Canada" Sciascia was a Bronx-based capo in charge of the Bonanno family's Sicilian faction. Sciascia also was the key connection to the Bonanno's outpost in Canada, which the Mafia Commission had placed under Joseph Bonanno's purview back in the 1930s. Massino held a special interest in the Montreal faction going back to the 1980s. Vito Rizzuto ran the Montreal faction of the Bonannos, but was boss of his own crime family. At the time, it was unlikely Massino knew how powerful Rizzuto truly was.

Authors Adrian Humphreys and Lee Lamothe have written a nonfiction account of the Rizzuto Mafia family in Canada, The Sixth Family: The Collapse of the New York Mafia and the Rise of Vito Rizzuto, which posits that Rizzuto was in fact running what should be viewed as the Sixth Family. Rizzuto eventually stopped considering himself subservient to the Bonanno crime family in New York. However, as this book will explain, there was no formal break following the execution of Sciascia as has been widely postulated, according to Cicale. In fact, Cicale knows the amounts of two "tributes" Rizzuto sent to New York.

Sciascia had earned the animosity of Massino by complaining about another family capo—one then in Massino's good graces—Anthony "TG" Graziano, father of the women responsible for the VH1 reality TV show "Mob Wives." Sciascia, always known for his outspokenness, had charged that the Staten Island-based mobster was liberally dipping into his own drug supply. This happened after one meeting involving Sciascia, Vitale and Graziano. Sciascia noticed that a glassy-eyed Graziano was unable to follow the discussion and was also unsteady on his feet. Sciascia was literally stunned. He talked about it with Vitale afterward, when the two were alone.

"TG is a captain," Gerlando said, alarmed.

"You're supposed to be representing your family and you're walking around high? You're going to other, outside families and making a fool of yourself? It reflects on the family. Every time I see this guy, he is stoned."

Vitale, who in testimony told of his fondness for George, met with Massino soon afterward and conveyed Sciascia's message, which appeared to arouse Massino's suspicions enough for him to actually make inquiries of Graziano regarding Sciascia's allegations. But Massino also was fond of Graziano and considered him a personal friend. So when Graziano swore on his "children's eyes" that he was not indulging in narcotics and that Sciascia had merely witnessed side effects caused by a prescription stomach medication that Graziano was consuming, Massino decided to believe him. Massino quickly sent word to George, who nevertheless still kept away from Graziano. That wasn't the only black mark against Sciascia's name, however. The Sicilian quick to shoot off his mouth—or his gun— supposedly also had ripped into the brother of the Bonanno family's previous boss, Philip "Rusty" Rastelli, complaining about a debt that Rusty's brother insisted George owed him. In fact, Sciascia confronted the brother, named Marty, telling him, "You got nothing coming. I'm going to war tomorrow if you want."

Nestled in the friendly atmosphere of Amici's, Sal knew the apparent reasons for Massino's order to whack Sciascia. Still, he couldn't hide the shock evident in his facial expression, which prompted Massino to snap: "If you have any problems with that, I'll get other people. I don't need you."

Vitale, who would later say "George was a good man," threw his hands in the air. "Whatever you want to do, Joe," he said.

Any other response likely would've meant that Massino would be whispering in the ear of another ranking member that "Sal has got to go." A Mafia boss's words have the inviolability of a papal bull. Vitale once had the power himself during Massino's incarceration from the mid-1980s through 1992, as well as for the next two years, when a paroled Massino was disallowed freedom of movement to meet his criminal cohorts in public. But now Massino had six years of true freedom under his prodigious belt. And he had not shown much gratitude to his brother-in-law, who by then may have perceived his eventual marginalization within the crime family, which contributed to a drop in his standing—as well as his income.

Vitale wasn't alone in how he felt toward George, according to Cicale, who said there was an additional reason why Massino ordered George's death.

"George was a great guy and no one had a bad word to say about him," Cicale said. "The boss started to see that and felt it was time to punch George's ticket. Truth be told, Joe Massino never liked it when someone within his crime family was gaining popularity. So Joe's way of dealing with that issue was to kill the person. End of story."

Massino told Vitale to contact Patrick "Patty From the Bronx" DeFilippo, another Bonanno capo, to arrange the hit. Massino had already spoken to Patty two weeks earlier, he told Vitale. Anthony "Tony Green" Urso, another Bonanno capo, was storing a silencer-equipped pistol. (The gun, however, was not used in the hit—and turned up years later in surprising circumstances). TG Graziano was also available if Patty needed help getting a van or car in which to pull off the hit, added Massino, revealing his Machiavellian deviousness.

Graziano was the capo George accused of sniffing family product. Additionally, Patty was in the midst of an ongoing business dispute with George and would benefit monetarily once the Sicilian was out of the way. As a reward, Massino also erased a loan DeFilippo owed him, telling Vitale to rip Patty's page out of the loanshark book and tear it into little pieces.

The body was to be dumped on the street in the Bronx. Let the police puzzle over what would appear to be a street crime. George had been a drug merchant all his life and Massino knew that his narcotics background would keep the police busy (and it did for years, in fact). Massino planned to distance the Bonanno family, including its boss, from the hit. Word would be put out for everyone to attend the wake as a show of strength and respect—but really as a strategy to confuse the inquisitive.

Obviously, Massino didn't want to attract law enforcement scrutiny, but he didn't want George's crew in New York or Montreal (Massino believed that he was dealing with a capo who had a crew in both cities) to get any ideas either. Massino thought that Rizzuto, the mobster in Montreal about whom he knew little, would be a good replacement for George. However, Vito would turn down Massino's offer of becoming captain. According to Cicale's information though, Vito's split from New York may have been personally aimed at Massino, the man who murdered his childhood friend. George also was Rizzuto's man in New York. All things considered, the fewer who knew the truth, the better, as far as Joe Massino was concerned. Vitale, Massino noted, was charged with overall responsibility for the hit;

Sal was to ensure the murder was successfully carried out. Massino himself wouldn't even be in New York—or the United States for that matter.

The very next morning Joe was flying with his wife to a tropical island vacation. "Try to get it done before I come home," Massino said.

There was at least one other meeting that Massino had regarding George from Canada. Massino took the pulse of an up-and-coming Bronx-based soldier named Vincent "Vinny Gorgeous" Basciano, according to Cicale.

Vinny Gorgeous actually hated that moniker, derived from the name of a beauty salon he'd opened after his video store went bust.

"No one ever called him "Vinny Gorgeous" to his face," Cicale said.

Basciano, a slick, well-groomed mobster earning a fortune on the street from drugs and gambling, among other things, was also smart, loyal to Massino, and strong, never to shirk the gun or the knife.

Massino summoned him to meet at an Italian restaurant not-so-secretly owned by the Bonanno boss. Casa Blanca Restaurant, in Maspeth, Queens, was ostensibly owned by a Bonanno soldier but all family members knew who really owned it. Massino had assumed off-the-books ownership of the blue-collar eatery in 1996. It was a public place, so Massino didn't fear the negative connotations associated with Mafia social clubs (he had in fact banned all social clubs, among other things, to help insulate him and members of the crime family).

Casa Blanca could seat up to 80 diners, bathing them in neon lighting. The eatery, named after the classic 1942 film Casablanca, featured a life-sized statue of Humphrey Bogart himself, resplendent in white dinner jacket, at the front entrance. The menu was loaded with Sicilian and Southern Italian cuisine. As Cicale noted, "Joe held court there, sitting in the back wearing a warm-up suit with a pack of Marlboro cigarettes on the table. At their meeting, Joe asked Vinny how he liked George, how George was doing, and so on."

Massino hardly needed to spell out his intentions to Vinny, who sized up the situation at once.

"Vinny informed me about the questions the boss had asked him, and schooled me too. He told me that when the boss asks you questions like that, he is asking for a reason. He wants to see your reaction. So be extremely careful. Because if you tell the boss, 'I love that person and I would die for him,' then if it's the wrong person, that just might happen."

Vinny was a good friend to George, but he was also a true gangster at heart, so friendship aside, Vinny figured he might as well earn off the unknowingly doomed Sicilian capo, Cicale said. "Vinny knew it was only a matter of time before George's ticket was punched, so he started calling George every day to borrow money, knowing George would never collect the debt. All in all, Vinny borrowed $265,000 right before George was clipped."

Shortly after obtaining Massino's edict, Vitale met with DeFilippo on Manhattan's tony East Side, where DeFilippo had an apartment on York Avenue. The two engaged in a walk-talk. "You know what we gotta do," Vitale said.

"I'm all set up," Patty replied.

"You need a car? I can get you a car," Vitale offered.

Patty didn't need a car. He had to tell Vitale that twice. Vitale pressed him for more details, asking how the hit on George would go down. "I'm gonna kill him in Johnny Joe's truck," Patty replied.

That was John "Johnny Joe" Spirito, a Bonanno soldier. Cicale has said that the hit on George from Canada was "a classic Mafia set up."

The plan was to lure George into the city so that he and Patty could sit down and resolve their business dispute. DeFilippo wanted Johnny Joe there to pick up George and bring him to the "meeting" because George was familiar with Spirito's white SUV. DeFilippo wanted to use a car that Sciascia would be familiar with. Building a false comfort zone around the man was essential; just the right touch to preoccupy him for the needed moment to end his life. George from Canada was a professional killer, among other things, so he wouldn't walk blindly into a trap. Massino's men had to prepare themselves for a guy who could very well pull out a pistol and shoot them before they fired their volley at him. The body would be dumped on the street in the Bronx, as Massino had requested. As a safety measure, Patty told Vitale that Michael "Mikey Nose" Mancuso would follow them in his Nissan as a backup shooter.

Vitale seemed content with what he'd heard. There was one last item of business to take care of, however. The next day, the two met again so Vitale could equip Patty with two guns and a silencer, procured from "Tony Green." The last thing a mobster wants is a new gun if he's organizing a murder. Even Patty, not the most experienced killer in the crime family, knew that much. Hits need to go down like clockwork, precise and swift. No professional killer ever wants to pull a new gun and fire it cold into a target. A new gun could jam and misfire, causing the wrong guys to die. So Patty asked: "Does it work? Did you try it?"

"No," Sal replied.

Patty hopped into a car and Sal drove through midtown Manhattan. DeFilippo held the gun in the air through an open sunroof and fired off several rounds. Cicale noted that DeFilippo had been impressed with the silencer on the 9 millimeter weapon. "All Patty heard was the "pfft" of air blowing out the barrel," Cicale recalled. "The shells ejecting out the side of the gun made a louder noise than the firing of the gun. The weapon was sweet, Fat Patty later told me."

Vitale pulled over to the curb grabbing Patty to get his attention before the two parted that night. "Joe told me to tell you: Hit him high, hit him low."

That meant shoot him in both the head and the body, alternating the shots. "I got it," Patty said. "Don't worry."

The hit was planned and scheduled; George Sciascia was a walking dead man. The rest was just detail. Still, the hit on George didn't go down precisely the way Vitale and Massino had planned.

# 3 ZIPS IN THE BONANNO FAMILY

George Sciascia was born in Cattolica Eraclea in Sicily, also the birthplace of Vito Rizzuto. The two were raised side by side, living only houses away in the small rural town founded in medieval times and located some 50 miles south of Palermo, the 2700-year-old Sicilian capitol.

Sciascia journeyed to North America with Rizzuto and other young male members of the Sicilian Cosa Nostra looking to mint their fortune in the drug trade. Sciascia chose to live in the U.S. In 1958, at 24, he immigrated to America as a stowaway, according to the Justice Department, which nevertheless granted him an immigration visa. After bouncing around in New Jersey and Queens, George eventually took up residence in the Bronx with his family and remained there until his death.

Sciascia drifts on and off the radar. Years of his life in America are unaccounted for. "We didn't know enough about George," a U.S. law enforcement analyst told Lamothe and Humphreys. "There were a thousand Georges," he added, referring to the vast number of Sicilian men, mostly young, tied to the drug trade and Cosa Nostra life after immigrating to America.

Many arrived in New York and New Jersey and had a lot of free time on their hands. Salvatore "Toto" Catalano is among the thousands of "Georges." Born in 1941 in the rural Sicilian town of Ciminna, he and his two brothers were sent to America in 1966 by Sicilian traffickers who had taken over the former French Connection operation. Bosses of the Sicilian Cosa Nostra wanted Catalano and the others to infiltrate the American Mafia. Catalano, a burly man with a thick neck, lived quietly and ostensibly worked as a baker and shopkeeper on Knickerbocker Avenue. A made member of the Bonanno family as well as the Sicilian Cosa Nostra, he was in America to build franchises for Sicilian traffickers to use for selling and distributing heroin to members of the American Mafia and others.

13

Catalano considered Carmine "Lilo" Galante, former underboss to Joe Bonanno, to be a key resource for contacts and protection for the heroin business. Catalano and those with him established an infrastructure to facilitate dealing and distribution: pizzerias and bakeries (hence, the Pizza Connection name). Historically, it is believed that Galante brought Sicilians here to act as his muscle to help him assume control of the drug trade in New York. Catalano and some other Zips, including Baldo Amato and César Bonventre, were part of the Sicilian trafficking operation, which was separate from the traditional Bonanno drug trafficking operation through Montreal. The Catalano operation started to receive inquiries from Gaetano Badalamenti, the former head of the Sicilian Cosa Nostra Commission, who had fled to Brazil after he was driven out of Sicily by the murderous Corleonese faction when it assumed control of the Commission following a bloody Mafia war in the early 1970s. Badalamenti, at the time the most-wanted narcotics trafficker in the world, had established a major drug operation in the American Midwest using blood relatives working in pizzerias to sell and distribute the heroin he shipped to them. Apparently, he wanted to sell drugs to the Catalano Zip faction in New York. So ultimately the Pizza Connection Case involved Catalano and other select Bonanno Zips working for both the Sicilian traffickers and Badalamenti, who inadvertently clashed head-on into law enforcement's massive net.

The FBI began investigating Catalano and his group in New York following the Carmine Galante slaying. The investigation grew into one of the longest and most complex organized crime cases in history and ultimately involved the FBI, DEA, NYPD and U.S. Customs working in close cooperation with the Italian National Police and Swiss authorities. This marked an unprecedented breakthrough for U.S. and Italian law enforcement authorities in the fight against the Mafia. Officials from both countries shared highly sensitive information. Arrests were coordinated in the U.S., Italy, Switzerland and Spain on April 9, 1984, following the capture of Badalamenti and several family members the previous day in Madrid, Spain. Perhaps fittingly, the Pizza Connection investigation culminated in one of the longest organized crime trials in history. The final indictment was filed in February of 1985 and charged 35 defendants with conspiracy to import drugs and evade banking and money laundering statutes, but the operation itself was said to have included more than 200 participants.

Bonventre, good friends with Amato, didn't live to stand trial. The enterprise had shipped around $1.6 billion worth of heroin to the U.S. between 1975 and 1984. Sciascia, though a member of the Bonanno's Zip faction, appears not to have been involved in the Catalano operation and was not part of the Pizza Connection case. He did get nabbed in a Gambino family drug case, the same one that sent John Gotti's brother,

Gene, away for decades. Sciascia fled the country but eventually returned and faced a separate, later trial and won an acquittal, though it was later learned a juror was bribed.

By the mid 1970s, Sciascia was established in the Mafia, belonging to the then-burgeoning faction of Sicilians of the Bonanno family. By 1981, he was already a capo in the family. He traveled to Canada frequently and had forged close ties to the Bonanno crew in Montreal, headed by personal friend Rizzuto. George from Canada was the natural liaison between the New York family and its crew in Montreal, officially established in the 1950s. In 1981, Sciascia was among the Bonanno members who helped murder three dissident capos: Alphonse "Sonny Red" Indelicato, Dominick "Big Trin" Trinchera and Philip "Phil Lucky" Giaccone.

Swaggering, charismatic Sonny Red had grown too strong and cocky. He'd shown blatant disrespect toward Rastelli and Massino, as well as the Sicilian members of the family. Nicknamed for a pair of custom-made red-colored leather cowboy boots he always wore, Sonny Red also was personally strong and prone to violence. He once drove an ice pick through a man's chest with such force it punched through the floor, requiring the use of a tire iron to pry the body free. He served 12 years in Sing Sing penitentiary for a 1951 shooting in a social club that left one man dead and the other wounded. The survivor identified Sonny Red, who was released from prison in 1966 and placed on lifetime parole due to his heavy involvement with the Mafia and narcotics trafficking. Sonny Red built a strong power base over the next 15 years that included at least four capos, each of whom commanded between six to twelve soldiers (and related associates). All of them were tired of Rastelli's leadership, or lack thereof. Sonny Red also had significant ties to all five families, particularly high-level members of the violent Colombo family (Indelicato was under investigation for the murder of Crazy Joe Gallo when he was killed). Vincent "The Chin" Gigante also supported him.

Big Trin, Giaccone and some other captains would've gone along with anything Sonny Red wanted, lining them up directly against the official boss, Rastelli, backed by Joe Massino and other capos, including Dominick "Sonny Black" Napolitano, who'd been Rastelli's acting boss for a time. The Zips—which consisted of Sciascia, as well as Catalano, Amato and Bonventre—briefly were considered a separate faction but eventually joined Massino and Napolitano over their concern regarding Sonny Red controlling the family. One decisive factor was that Sonny Red had stiffed some of them by refusing to pay for a consignment of heroin that Sciascia had fronted him.

Of the 15 or so Bonanno capos then in power, who controlled about 150 soldiers altogether, yet another faction established itself. This one was composed mostly of old timers—including Salvatore "Sally Fruits"

Ferrugia, Stefano "Stevie Beef" Cannone, and Nicholas "Nicky Glasses" Marangello—were waiting on the sidelines until one group won. The Bonanno crime family was not benefitting from the leadership of Rastelli, who spent most of his term as boss in prison. The truth was the family was continuing a decline begun in 1965 with the ousting of founder Joseph Bonanno, who was allowed to live but was exiled from New York for his machinations against Commission bosses Carlo Gambino, who was the de facto boss of bosses, and Thomas "Tommy Three-Fingers Brown" Lucchese. The once renowned crime family was thrown into a tailspin due to a lack of leadership. Without a strong boss on the street, the family was unable to show strength at sit-downs and at Commission meetings (something that mattered less once the family lost its seat following the Donnie Brasco infiltration). Furthermore, Rastelli was personally not management material. He was not popular with many Mafiosi on the street and was unable to rally the troops. In fact, for all the support Massino gave Rastelli, Big Joey even complained about him, once telling Vitale: "How smart can he be? He spent half his life in jail."

Cicale noted that Rastelli spent part of his final prison stint in the same prison as Massino and that the two had little to do with each other. When Rastelli tried desperately to regain his Commission seat, he was flatly refused. Anthony "Fat Tony" Salerno was one of Rusty's formidable obstacles.

On May 22, 1984, at his bugged Palma Boys Social Club, Salerno met with Mathew "Matty the Horse" Ianniello, a capo in the Genovese family, and soldier James Ida when the subject of Rastelli and the Commission arose.

Rastelli relied too heavily on "junk guys," Salerno said. "Listen, we don't recognize [Rastelli] down there… I didn't want to meet with [Rastelli], Paul [Castellano] didn't want to meet. Tony Ducks told Rusty," Salerno continued: "'Listen,'" he said, "'Take care of your family first. Straighten out your family and when you straighten them out, then we talk about the Commission.'"

At another meeting, with Luchese family underboss Salvatore "Tom Mix" Santoro and consiglieri Christopher "Christie Tick" Furnari, Salerno expressed concern that Rastelli's over-the-top narcotics business endangered the entire New York Mafia.

# 4  MAN OF STEEL V. MEN OF COPPER

Back in the early 1970s through 1980s, the Canadian drug spigot spewed a colossal flow of narcotics for eager buyers seeking to make their fortunes by distributing drugs throughout the United States. A boss was needed to control and organize the business for the Bonannos, which had built the pipeline. The lack of such a figure caused many homicides in gangland over a spate of years, mainly because there was so much competition for the position of boss of the Bonanno family.

The combination of a weak, imprisoned and ineffective Rastelli and the availability of a seemingly endless flow of low-priced quality wholesale heroin would provide the man in control untold wealth. Sonny Red was ready, willing and able to seize control of the Bonanno family. Then something happened that reunited the factions, however briefly. That something—someone, really—was named Carmine Galante. No one could accuse the murdering Mafia strong man and former underboss to Joe Bonanno himself of not having the right stuff to be boss. Linked to more than 80 gangland murders, he stood a mere 5-foot-4, though there was "power and little compunction packed into his wiry… frame," noted Humphreys in his book, The Enforcer: Johnny Pops Papalia: A Life and Death in the Mafia. Utterly fearless, Galante—of whom an NYPD lieutenant famously said: "The rest of them are copper; he is pure steel"— was among the first to recognize the importance of Canada as a drug smuggling route into the U.S. He had, in fact, gone to Montreal in 1953 at the age of 43 and had literally organized the region's criminal activity for boss Joe Bonanno.

"He was a very motivated and motivating man," Humphreys wrote in The Enforcer, "and his organizing drive in Montreal was alarmingly thorough."

Backing Galante was a gang of strong enforcers led by Frank Petrula,

17

who helped cultivate Bonanno's initial interest in Montreal. But fueling Bonanno's immediate personal concern were the 100 bookies who had fled to Montreal to escape litigation created in wake of the 1950-1951 televised "Kefauver Committee." Galante went up there to tell them that although they had departed New York, they were still beholden to the Bonanno crime family. In Galante's grip, Montreal "wept and bled," Humphreys wrote. Every nightclub and brothel, even underground abortionists, was shaken down by Galante and Petrula, who shared a sadistic streak. Humphreys relates a story about the two forcing a busboy in one establishment to dance barefoot atop crushed glass.

Galante brought organized crime in Montreal under his purview, but his wandering eye quickly sized up and remained forever focused on the opportunities Montreal afforded heroin trafficking. It was where drug wholesalers from Europe could meet with American and Canadian dealers to make their trafficking arrangements. The Mafia—particularly the Bonannos, straddling both countries—enjoyed supremacy in the heroin trade; they wholesaled the diluted heroin to dealers in major cities throughout the U.S. As Alexander Hortis noted in The Mob and the City: The Hidden History of How the Mafia Captured New York, their heroin was "superior" due to [the mob's] overseas connections in the underworld.

The Mafia was supplied with heroin by the Sicilian Cosa Nostra working with crime families based on the French Island of Corsica. The Corsicans were culturally similar to the families of the Sicilian Cosa Nostra. Although they were French, they even spoke in an Italian dialect. From the port city of Marseilles, the Corsicans ran smuggling operations throughout the Mediterranean. The heroin they refined was created out of the rich opium grown in the fields of Turkey and Lebanon. The heroin proved easier to smuggle by air into New York from Montreal. Nevertheless, this was only one of a seemingly infinite number of "pipelines" into the U.S. Drug deals are opportunistic in nature. Smugglers will bring drugs to the world's premiere market in any way possible. For a period of time though, the pipeline from Montreal proved to be immensely profitable for the Bonanno family.

Galante was so tempted by heroin's deadly dollar signs he sought permanent resident status in Canada in February 1954, using as his reason a token investment in a Canadian restaurant. He revoked his own request when Montreal officials were poised to investigate him for procedural reasons. Galante at the time was suspected of killing an NYPD member as well as an influential journalist of Italian descent. He yanked his application so as to not permanently scotch his opportunity. Galante went back to America, and Bonanno appointed a two-man panel to oversee the family's interests in Montreal. By 1960, Galante was sleeping in a prison cell, having been convicted for belonging to a massive heroin trafficking ring that included gangsters on both sides of the border. Galante may have been a mental dullard with a low IQ but he possessed a long memory. Galante announced his intentions shortly before his release in 1974 by ordering his men to dynamite the entrance of Frank "The Prime Minister" Costello's mausoleum to herald his return to the streets. Once he'd regained his freedom, a bald and bespectacled Galante immediately threw his weight around. Refusing to acknowledge the imprisoned Rastelli as boss of the family, Galante assumed control and ramped up narcotics importation. Galante also enforced a tax on Sicilians operating in the U.S. He refused to share a dime with other bosses. Instead, Galante created a sort of Praetorian Guard out of Sicilian gunmen whom he himself inducted into the crime family. He also made traditional Italian-Americans into Bonanno family members. The solemn right to induct members is fundamentally reserved for a boss. Galante's greed caused his downfall. That and the fact that he was seen as the mastermind behind the murders of at least eight members of the Gambino family and perhaps members of other crime families as part of his efforts to consolidate his hold over the drug business.

Bosses tend to be hesitant about killing another boss. But they will certainly hasten the effort when the intended target fails to repay a loan or withholds their perceived cut of the proceeds. Carlo Gambino, who in 1957 seized control of the crime family that still carries his name, didn't hesitate to take out a Genovese boss named Thomas "Tommy Ryan" Eboli. (Eboli was only a front boss for Philip "Benny Squint" Lombardo, the true boss of the Genovese family from the late 1960s through the early 1980s, although no one would know this until decades later.) In 1972, Eboli was living on borrowed time and the gruff mobster didn't seem to care. Gambino and other bosses on the Commission had given him $4 million to fund a drug deal that went south when the narcotics merchant was busted and sent away to prison for 20 to life. The bosses lost millions of dollars and Tommy Ryan, unbelievably, not only failed to repay the debt but refused even to acknowledge it. Gambino ordered Eboli's murder the same year. The Mafia hitters purposely waited until Tommy Ryan was departing his mistress's house, versus arriving, before shooting him dead. Owing to his status, Gambino thought the man at least deserved to go out with a smile on his face.

Galante, however, won no concessions. On a terribly hot and humid July day in 1979, he had finished lunch on the back patio of Joe and Mary's Italian-American Restaurant with several others, including his Sicilian bodyguards, when three men wearing ski masks showed up and blasted Galante and two dining companions to death in one of the most brutal gangland slayings. Galante's death was immortalized in an iconic photo taken by an enterprising photographer. In it, the once-fearsome gangster is sprawled on his back, one eye gone, a cigar still in his mouth.

A deliveryman witnessed the fleeing masked assassins, reportedly Sonny Red, his son Bruno and Big Trin. One barked at him: "Get the fuck out of here or I'll kill you."

Sonny Red was the true power behind the Galante hit, Cicale affirmed. "Massino and Rastelli may have spoken to the Commission for approval, but the hit on Galante was put together by Sonny Red, who put his son Anthony 'Bruno' Indelicato in charge. Actually, right after Galante was taken out, Bruno was rewarded with a promotion in rank to Bonanno crime family capo," Cicale said.

Bruno is among the group of Bonannos serendipitously caught on FBI surveillance footage later that very same day hugging and kissing Gambino underboss Aniello "Neal" Dellacroce at his social club the Ravenite in New York's Little Italy.

Cicale noted that some Mafia members had disagreed with the decision to hit Galante. This group believed Galante was, in fact, doing right by the Bonanno crime family. He was stepping in to fill a void that needed filling.

"Galante was becoming a powerhouse and was one tough mobster who was putting the Bonanno crime family back on the map, and all the other New York crime families knew this," Cicale said. "That is the real reason why Galante was killed on Commission approval."

"Galante was claiming what belonged to the Bonanno crime family and there was nothing the other crime families could do about it. Galante was correct in his actions, so they decided to plot against him, setting him up to be killed. That was told to me by a Genovese crime boss," Cicale noted.

Less than three years later, another insurrection was brewing within the Bonanno family, with Sonny Red and his capos at the helm of the opposition. Indelicato, backed by massive firepower, actually grew somewhat reluctant about causing a civil war, which would have disrupted business for all the New York families. Sonny Red was willing to sit down with Massino and other Rastelli loyalists to reach a compromise. A meeting was set for May 5, 1981, at Brooklyn's Embassy Terrace, which was actually owned by Gambino member Salvatore "Sammy the Bull" Gravano. According to a Bonanno capo who was with Indelicato and capos Frank Lino, Giaccone, and Trinchera before they left for the meeting, Indelicato said, "If there is shooting, everybody is on their own. Try to get out."

On that same night, Sonny Red reportedly scattered his crews throughout New York City in case the other faction decided to take them all out in one strike. Several Bonanno members supposedly stayed with Tommy "Karate" Pitera while the three capos were slaughtered.

Cicale related the often-retold story with a slightly different spin: "Sonny Red was gunned down along with two other Bonanno family captains. They were all set to meet Joe Massino, but it was actually a trap. It was a power move that allowed Massino to take full control of the Bonanno crime family—and none other than John Gotti had been whispering in Joe's ear to move. With Joe on the fast track, Gotti knew he'd be able to control him and that would make Gotti's position in his crime family stronger."

Gotti's Gambino family crew provided assistance by assuming responsibility for body disposal—and then failed to do an adequate job. Sonny Red's corpse was found jutting out of a lot in Queens, New York within one week of the hit. Big Trin and Phil Lucky, however, were buried deeper and remained underground for decades.

Massino initially wanted an additional body to be buried as well. "Bruno was supposed to be there that evening," Cicale said. "Joe Massino knew that Bruno could be a threat so they expected he'd be at the meeting so they could take him out too. But Bruno was instructed to stay back. His father told him that if something happened to him and Big Trin and Phil, then Bruno was supposed to kill Joe Massino."

Bruno never avenged his father's death. In fact, he tried to go into hiding. "He's my pal, and I have fond memories of him, but he sure as hell dogged that one," Cicale said. "He totally blew off his father's wishes. Bruno was also a stone-cold cocaine addict. Everyone in the crime family was well aware of it but no one had dared to say a word for fear of Sonny Red, Bruno's father."

So Bruno fell through the cracks and avoided the hit on his life put in place by Massino.

"What also saved Bruno was our wonderful federal government. Bruno was arrested and did his time, which made him even less of a concern to Massino," added Cicale.

In organizing the hit, Massino reached out to Canada for the shooters. Vito Rizzuto arrived with two additional members of the Canadian faction: Emanuele Ragusa and the "old timer," whose name has been lost to history. It is believed the old man was an associate of Vito's father, Nicolo, there to personally see how young Vito comported himself.

Rizzuto and his crew were the primary shooters, according to Vitale, who noted that he and George Sciascia were designated backup shooters. Sciascia also served as the escort, walking the three capos into the basement ambush. Once inside, Sciascia signaled the start of the attack by slowly running his fingers through his slick pompadour. Rizzuto and company then burst out of a closet and opened fire. Amid all the bloody pandemonium, Sciascia leaped at the opportunity to put one right in Sonny Red's head. The fatal shot was retribution for Indelicato refusing to pay Sciascia the $1.5 million he owed for the consignment of heroin.

After the successful hit—no small feat, killing three capos at once—Sciascia and Rizzuto became firmly entrenched in Massino's good graces.

# 5  THE CLASSIC MAFIA HIT

Nevertheless, as early as 1995, Sciascia possibly sensed impending doom. That year, he tried to officially move with his family to Canada, but his request for Canadian citizenship was denied due to his criminal background. He had just beaten a major narcotics case tied to the Gambino family (the trial had been fixed, as noted), but Canadian immigration officials considered his lengthy criminal file and even queried him in person before deciding it would be preferential for Canada that he not join its citizenry.

George from Canada was a citizen of Italy and a permanent resident in the U.S. George from Canada was not really "from Canada" at all. Four years later, Sciascia was set up for his own death. It would prove to be Massino's final murder in a Mafia career that was long and bloody. On the morning of March 18, 1999, the last day of his life, "George got his usual check-in call from Vinny," Cicale noted, adding that George then received, in quick succession, another call from "the grim reaper, Fat Patty."

Sciascia took the calls at his headquarters, Throggs Neck Jewelers, located on East Tremont Avenue. One of his relatives ran the place. "We will work out our differences," Patty said, intending to convey a mood of reconciliation, then requested that George meet him that evening.

Sciascia apparently hadn't the slightest inkling of the deadly wheels set in motion. He casually noted on a slip of paper the location of the meet and slipped it into his wallet.

"John 'Johnny Joe' Spirito and Patty were already locked and loaded but had to wait for Michael 'Mikey Nose' Mancuso, who in the end dogged it and never showed up," said Cicale. "What a fucking punk. That alone could have easily gotten the 'Nose' killed, but Fat Patty loved Michael and saved his ass when the boss finally asked why 'Mikey Nose' hadn't been there."

Continuing, Cicale said, "Mikey Nose was always a punk. How could a made man walk around the neighborhood strutting his shit and say hello to the man who murdered his own father?" Cicale was referring to old claims that Mancuso's father was gunned down by a Bronx street thug who "everyone knew." Mancuso's father, Cicale related, "was with Arnold "Zeke" Squitieri and Alfonse "Funzi" Sisca, Gambino associates at the time, when Mancuso's father met his demise. The three had been partying one night, drinking and sniffing cocaine. What great pals [Zeke and Funzi were]... They watch their friend get killed and didn't do a fucking thing about it...Two more fucking punks."

Cicale recalled that Mancuso had a tendency to become scarce when "heavy lifting" had to be done. "Mikey always made some type of lame excuse when called upon to help with a piece of work. He'd say: 'There's too many people around' or 'I don't know where he lives.'"

Mikey's failure to arrive did not put the hit on hold, however. "As Johnny Joe and Fat Patty pull up to the meeting location, George is already standing next to his car," said Cicale. "Fat Patty pulls the minivan over and tells George to get in. Johnny Joe opens the passenger side door, greets George and offers him the front seat as he nonchalantly hopped in back, behind George. Sciascia wouldn't have blinked at that, taking it as a sign of respect. Sciascia was a captain, after all, and Johnny Joe just a soldier. Johnny Joe took his seat behind George in the back of the minivan and just as the door swung shut, he raised a .25 caliber gun to George's head. Johnny Joe let loose seven quick gun shots, the roar causing Johnny Joe's and Patty's ears to painfully ring for some time. The two had previously decided that the silencer-equipped 9 millimeter was too powerful to use in an automobile."

Blood and gore splashed on the dashboard, the windshield and the passenger-side window. The .25 caliber slugs fired into Sciascia's body had penetrated his brain and torso, causing blood to fill the car where George had been seated. Patty had never even put the car into drive.

After the fireworks were over and the smoke cleared, Johnny Joe opened the back door, walked to the front passenger side, opening the door where the lifeless body of George from Canada sat slumped over the dashboard. Johnny Joe reached in, grabbed George by the shoulders and pulled his lifeless body out of the car. The corpse landed with a thud on the blacktop pavement of the deserted street. Sciascia lay there until the police found him. His silver pompadour was bloodied; his body was still clad in the red-and-black sweater, gray dress pants and black shoes he'd worn to the "reconciliation" meeting. After the mission was accomplished, Johnny Joe returned to the back seat and Fat Patty put the vehicle in drive. The two men still had a lot of work to do. First, get rid of the gun; then drive the car to Queens so it could be chopped up. When law enforcement was finally able to ID George, they realized they had a high-ranking member of one of the Five Families in the morgue. But they hadn't the slightest inkling of who was behind the murder or why.

Investigators reportedly puzzled over the murder for years, as Massino had intended. One piece of evidence (Sciascia's handwritten note to himself regarding the location of the meeting that he'd placed in his wallet) did not help them. Massino's duplicity continued.

"The word put on the street was that George was killed in a robbery or a drug deal that went bad. Vito from Canada was not buying it one bit. He refused to replace George as captain. Other stories started to trickle down to Joe Massino," Cicale said. "He did not like what he was hearing so he immediately sent for Vito to get his ass down to Maspeth, Queens, in New York where Joe informed Vito who the boss was and that Canada was still under the control of the Bonanno crime family."

Vito may not have agreed with what Joe Massino had said, but he listened. The monies still kept coming in from all the illegal activities in Canada, even after the murder of George Sciascia. Many have speculated that this is when Rizzuto's "Sixth Family" broke away from the Bonannos in New York and stopped paying tribute. This is not the case, according to Cicale. "Vito had no choice. If he did not show, he could have easily gotten killed—even by someone close to him in Canada. Keep in mind that everyone is always looking to move up in the ranks."

When informally contacted, a Canadian journalist and a "Sixth Family" specialist reported that Rizzuto had certainly tried to avoid traveling to the U.S., even booking flights that didn't connect in the U.S. When Rizzuto went to the U.S., he likely drove.

"Rizzuto carried out other orders issued from New York," Cicale said. "Massino, for example, sent word to Vito to open a strip club in Canada. Massino and Vito would be 50-50 partners. Vito did as he was told." Cicale believes the strip club episode was a test to see how Rizzuto responded.

When Rizzuto carried out Massino's wishes, Massino likely was content that whatever Rizzuto thought of the death of Sciascia, he was not planning anything that would represent any sort of threat to Massino or the Bonanno family's interests. And for the Mafia, strip clubs are great businesses—in many ways. Cash businesses are always handy, of course.

Testing his men was something Massino engaged in a lot, especially in the case of his savvier, higher-level guys. Cicale related a hypothetical story to provide perspective. "Let's say Vinny and I were with Joe at his restaurant and it was only the three of us. Now remember, everyone in the crime family's loyalty is to the boss. The boss is The Man.... The One... And if the boss tells you to keep something between you and him then that's where it stays, between you and him. End of Story. So, if I got up to go to the bathroom, Joe would look at Vinny and say: 'Vinny, keep this between the two of us, but that Dominick is a piece of shit. Be careful. I hear he is doing things behind the crime family's back. Remember, Vinny, this conversation does not leave this table. I know you like Dominick, but keep an eye on him.' Vinny would reply, 'Of course,' And then, later that evening, Vinny would excuse himself from the table and after Vinny was out of earshot, Joe would turn to me and say the same exact thing to me about Vinny, then tell me that this conversation was not to go any further. Joe always played everyone against one another. That's how he remained in power for over 25 years. So after the night was over Vinny and I headed back home to the Bronx, Vinny would tell me what Joe had said. We had his game and played along with him, because if Joe wanted to punch one of our tickets, Vinny and I knew what would have to be done. Joe Massino would be the one who would meet his maker. Vinny and I were brothers to the end and had each other's back. We had a special bond."

# 6  A BRIEF WORD ABOUT JOE

Joseph Bonanno was the founder of the Bonanno crime family, one of the
Five Families in New York.

He died in Tucson in May 2002, where he had been living for decades.
He was 97 and had outlasted all of his contemporaries—including such
gangsters as Salvatore Lucania, better known as Charles "Lucky" Luciano,
and other mobsters who helped organize crime in America in the 1930s.
Bonanno created a criminal empire in Brooklyn and slowly, steadily,
expanded it to include rackets in California, Arizona, and Canada. He was
the absolute ruler of his family from 1931 to the mid-1960s. Alone among
Mafia chieftains, he penned an autobiography, "A Man of Honor," that
was published in 1983. Bonanno likely later regretted the project. In the
book, Bonanno acknowledged has place among the founders of the "Mafia
Commission," the select group of mob bosses responsible for resolving
internal disputes among the 20 or so Mafia families or clans that had once
taken root in the U.S. The book planted the seeds in the mind of a young
Manhattan prosecutor who eventually created a criminal trial of the Mafia
Commission, involving the most powerful mobsters in New York.

Bonanno lived decades beyond the end of his formal Mafia career,
which began in New York during Prohibition. A youthful Bonanno was an
enforcer for Salvatore Maranzano. Bonanno later supported Maranzano's
efforts for supremacy during a deadly power struggle with a rival gang led
by Joseph "Joe the Boss" Masseria, known as the Castellammarese War. By
the early 1960s, Bonanno, who'd been named boss of his own family back
in the 1930s, had reaped huge profits from Mafia rackets including
gambling, loansharking and heroin trafficking. He also made millions
through legal investments in garment factories in New York City, a dairy
farm in upstate New York, cheese companies and real-estate investments.
Bonanno also made a fortune from an outpost cunningly established in

Canada—in Montreal, specifically. Bonanno's control up north was formalized by the American Mafia Commission in 1931, when it carved Canada up. Quebec, including Montreal, fell under the purview of Joseph Bonanno, while Southern Ontario, including the waterfront steelmaking town of Hamilton as well as Toronto were under the control of Bonanno's cousin, Stefano Magaddino, a powerful boss based in Buffalo, New York, who had a seat of his own on the Commission.

Canada consisted of various crime families who arrived from both the Sicilian Cosa Nostra and Calabrian 'Ndrangheta. The two groups historically worked together peacefully, though outbursts of violence occur, especially when the Rizzuto Cosa Nostra family gained hegemony in Quebec—and years later, especially in 2013, when Vito Rizzuto returned home from an American prison and turned loose a bloody vendetta the underworld probably hasn't seen since the 1930s to avenge the murders of both his father and his son. Hostilities are likely ongoing even today, after Vito's death in December 2013 from lung cancer. The distinction between Calabrian and Sicilian was less important to the American Mafia, which seems to have used the rivalry to manipulate the territory. That was Bonanno's strategy, anyway, in Montreal. The proud Sicilian protégé of Maranzano appointed a two-man panel to oversee his interests there; he favored 'Ndrangheta boss Vic Cotroni, and appointed the Sicilian Cosa Nostra boss Luigi Greco as Cotroni's lieutenant. Bonanno "gave Cotroni the edge," as Lamothe and Humphrey's reported. Bonanno's balance of power established decades of peace and prosperity. Despite the wide-ranging criminal rackets belonging to his empire, Bonanno was not once during his 30 years in power indicted for a crime.

Bonanno shunned the glitzy styles favored by other Mafiosi of his time and was hardly ever seen showboating in public. He preferred conducting Mafia business in private residences, especially his own home, or in one of the many rural retreats available to him and his compatriots. He also loved to cook sumptuous Italian feasts for his friends: pasta, veal, thick steaks—and the wine would flow. For a man who held dignity, honor and loyalty in such high regard, Bonanno's criminal career ended in the most ignoble of ways. He was unceremoniously expelled from the Mafia and exiled into retirement in Arizona when it was learned that he'd been plotting the murders of two of his fellow bosses—Thomas Lucchese and Carlo Gambino, both also progenitors of Mafia families still in place today.

Bonanno was seeking to solidify his position as the nation's dominant mob leader when his plotting backfired after a Profaci assassin, Joseph Colombo, who'd been assigned to organize the murders of Gambino and Lucchese, instead told Gambino. Bonanno then vanished for 19 months, claiming—once he resurfaced—that he'd been abducted. It is believed Bonanno reappeared when the other bosses, including the two he had marked for death, agreed to let him live. However, the agreement was that Bonanno would resign from his crime family and move to Arizona. In his self-justifying autobiography, Bonanno spun his foiled plotting in this manner: The bosses as well as members of his own family had become greedy; they no longer respected the Mafia's codes of behavior; and they even allowed in their ranks Italians who were not of Sicilian heritage. Many historians concluded that the Bonanno family never again reached the levels of wealth and power it had enjoyed when Joseph Bonanno was at the helm. However, an argument could be made that the family did see a return to power and fortune under Joseph Charles Massino, who took over as boss of the Bonanno crime family following the death of Phillip "Rusty" Rastelli.

# 7 MASSINO REINVENTS THE MAFIA

Massino is often called The Last Don because he was considered to be among the last of the clever, old-school dons, with enough juice on the street to be a de facto boss of bosses when he got out of prison in 1992.

At the time, many of the powerful mob bosses, including Gambino boss John Gotti and Luchese bosses Vittorio "Little Vic" Amuso and Anthony "Gaspipe" Casso had been arrested, with Genovese boss Vincent "The Chin" Gigante joining them in 1997. As for the Colombos, they had their own problems in the early 1990s as a street war erupted between two family factions, with one loyal to imprisoned boss Carmine "The Snake" Persico. The other faction was led by acting boss Victor "Little Vic" Orena, who actually had the majority of the capos on his side.

While Massino was away, the Bonanno family had fallen even deeper into disfavor due to its infiltration by FBI agent Joe Pistone using the name Donnie Brasco. As a result, the other New York families kicked them off the Commission. Thus, the Bonannos couldn't share in the large scale labor racketeering enterprises in which the other families were engaged. It later turned out to be the best thing that could have happened to the Bonannos. The family and its bosses were unscathed by the major racketeering trials of the 1980s—one of which focused on the Commission; and another focused on bid-rigging in the concrete industry. Many family members received life sentences.

Though Massino also was convicted in the 1980s, he was given a relatively short sentence. He was back on the street in 1992 and quickly worked to steadily revise and fortify the family and its rackets, looking to better insulate it, and himself, from law enforcement. Massino was 49 years old at the time and he saw a nice, fat stretch in front of him in which he planned to earn as much as possible while staying far away from the prying eyes of the feds and other law enforcement agencies that were focused on organized crime in New York. Massino shuttered family social clubs. He decentralized the structure of the family, turning crews into isolated cells. Information was no longer widely shared; it was parceled out on a need-to-know basis. Massino even stepped back from huge moneymaking schemes if they involved collaboration with another crime family. The Bonannos would go it alone, Massino told his men. He focused on the old standbys—loansharking and gambling—but also showed a more enterprising streak by starting up scams on Wall Street. On parole for two years, Massino also named Vitale his underboss; he could safely use his brother-in-law to run the family from afar. There was one significant meeting in November 1992, Selwyn Raab noted in Five Families. Massino met with all his capos in a hotel suite not far from JFK airport and told them about Vitale's role as underboss so Massino could finish his parole without ending up back in prison. Massino outlawed use of his name as part of his reorganization strategy. Members of the family were told to point or tug on their ear when referring to Massino so that no wiretap pinned anything to the boss. He even simplified the induction ceremony. He banned the use of all the usual accoutrements—no mass card, no gun or knife (in case the law raided an induction ceremony) and no more blood trickling out of a pricked finger. (Much later Massino sought to rechristen the crime family's name from Bonanno to Massino, though this gambit was short-lived.) Massino banned the use of cell phones and encouraged the men to propose their sons for membership, thinking this might keep any potential turncoats from straying. He created a war chest in which every Bonanno capo and soldier tossed in $100 a month to help pay the lawyers' expenses of members who were arrested.

Massino also got closer to the Sicilian faction of the family. He had brought the "Zips" into Rastelli's fold back in the early 1980s when he requested their help in putting down the potential insurrection by the three captains. As the Sicilians, who were based in Montreal and in New York, were largely off law enforcement's radar at the time, Massino planned to use them as a sort of private army. Massino had created a façade that he was a suburbanite living quietly with his family. He established a principal source of legitimate income through a catering service that he took over using Mafia leverage. He also secretly owned Casa Blanca. The greatest risk Massino took during what proved to be the final years of his career in the Mafia was ordering the murder of George from Canada. For a mobster who had so carefully hedged his exposure to law enforcement—actually, risk of any kind (he told his bookies to stop taking baseball bets because the unbeatable Yankees were eating into his revenue)—Massino left himself wide open when he put in motion the high-profile Sciascia hit that immediately caused organized crime investigators to ponder the ramifications and the context.

Also, Massino had committed the murder following passage of a law that later enabled prosecutors to seek the death penalty for the wily mob boss. It was known that George Sciascia had badmouthed TG Graziano. And Massino may have not liked the growing popularity of a gangster backed by the Montreal crew. One investigator, when the murder was first discovered, began to wonder if killing Sciascia was Massino's attempt to "clean house." After all, George from Canada went way back with Massino; had helped Massino in 1981 in the brutal, bloody murder of three men in a basement. Speaking years later, in April 2011, after he flipped, Massino testified about his reasoning for killing George. (That Massino failed three polygraph tests tends to cast doubt on the veracity of anything he says, however.)

"As much as I didn't want to kill him, I had to kill him," he told a defense lawyer on cross examination. The reason: George had disobeyed protocol, presumably by openly contesting TG Graziano's alleged drug addiction and not repaying a loan to a boss's brother.

# 8  TWO ZIPS REACT DIFFERENTLY

Salvatore "Sal the Iron Worker" Montagna held dual citizenship, in Italy and Canada, and was a soldier in the Bonanno crime family at the time of Massino's ascension to the top.

Montagna was born in Montreal in 1971 but raised in Sicily's infamous Castellammare del Golfo, where the crime family's progenitor and many original members hailed from. In the mid 1980s, at the age of 15, his family moved to the United States and settled in the Bronx. Little is known about his early years. Later, when he was named acting boss, Montagna married and lived in Elmont, a suburb on western Long Island near Queens. The couple had three daughters. Sal had previously started up a small metalworking company (earning him his nickname "Sal the Iron Worker") called Matrix Steel Co., located in Bushwick, Brooklyn, which is still in operation. During the late 1990s, Montagna's name was first overheard in wiretapped conversations between other members of the Bonanno crime family. Montagna was in an uncomfortable position following the hit on George from Canada. He belonged to the Bronx-based Sicilian faction of the family, which had been run by Sciascia. In addition, Montagna and Sciascia were close friends, according to Cicale. Massino didn't have to have a sit-down with Sal to know what was in his heart; the question for the calculating Massino was what Sal was thinking in his head. Montagna needed to be watched closely, Massino had decreed. Sal, however, well-schooled in the tenets of Cosa Nostra (he was a full-blooded Sicilian, after all), took the news in stride and seemed to digest it easy enough. Friendships are disposable in Cosa Nostra. Consider Vinny Basciano's actions upon hearing news of his friend's impending death. Sal held in check his emotions. He didn't react the way at least one other Sicilian had upon hearings news of the murder.

"They killed my goombah," Baldo Amato wept to Vitale, who had quickly arranged for a sit-down for the two at the Blue Bay Dinner on Frances Lewis Blvd., in Queens, New York.

"They did what?" Vitale replied. By playing dumb, he was assisting in the spinning of Massino's last murder. They talked, with Sal pretending to know even less than Amato.

"What the fuck is going on?" Vitale said at some point. "Baldo, wait for the boss [who was still on vacation] to come home. We'll discuss it with him. I don't know what's going on... I just don't know."

No one replaced George, Cicale said. The members of his crew were spread around to various capos. Montagna was specifically placed in Patty DeFilippo's crew so the trusted lieutenant could keep watch.

Of Massino's strategy with Montagna, Cicale said: "It was actually a wise move. Joe knew that he had Fat Patty's loyalty and who better to monitor Sal than Patty?"

Whatever Montagna's true feelings about the killing of his friend and boss, he kept his mouth shut. Sal didn't reveal what he was thinking to anyone. He did as he was told and complied with whatever Patty asked— never complaining, just serving as a loyal foot soldier in the Bonanno crime family. Following the murder, Patty began meeting with Massino every week at Casa Blanca; checking up on "The Iron Worker" was always one of the priorities.

"Joe made sure that he was aware of everything that was going on in the Bronx—just for a while, until things calmed down."

# 9 THE VINNY AND BRUNO SHOW

Relaxing, Dominick and his girlfriend were ensconced in the comforts of their private beachfront oasis. They shared a bottle of Barolo in the backyard of his home in the Throg's Neck section of the Bronx. The two were nestled close together as they enjoyed their private view of the Long Island Sound, as well as the night sky, in which the moon glowed above the cascades of lights outlining the Throg's Neck and Whitestone bridges.

It was a warm July night in 2001, and Dominick's mind was as far away from the mob as it could get when his pager suddenly lit up, vibrating on the top of a wooden table where it sat beside the bottle of wine. Dominick, who had been contemplating the fruits of his ties to the Bonanno crime family, moved with military precision when he saw the sequence of numbers displayed on his pager.

"I saw it was Vinny by the "711" that led a sequence of other numbers. We had created our own virtual language out of the numeric codes. Using our various pre-set sequence of digits, Vinny could tell me numerically where and when to meet him without ever saying a word. We were extremely cautious and made every effort never to slip up. We especially never wanted our words caught on tape. Twenty minutes later, I was on the streets of midtown Manhattan meeting Vinny and some other guy I had never seen before. They were sitting at a sidewalk café, drinking and talking. Vinny introduced me to the man he was with and the guy turned out to be a middle-aged Bonanno soldier from Canada. Vinny seemed to know him extremely well."

Dominick, however, didn't sit down with the men. Basciano told him to return to the Bronx

"I was instructed by Vinny to stop by our secret stash spot. A gym bag was stored there which contained something of high value. Vinny also handed me a piece of paper on which was scrawled a Manhattan street

34

address, where I was to meet another Bonanno soldier, also from Montreal. At that point I was told to give that second Bonanno soldier the gym bag. I was a loyal dog following the orders of my best friend and brother, so I immediately headed back into the Bronx. Twenty-five minutes later, I found myself entering the rented garage on Penny Field Avenue in Throg's Neck. That garage was the stash spot where all the drugs were stored. I did not want to draw any attention, so without turning on any lights, I opened the garage door, grabbed the gym bag of drugs stored in one of the back corners and headed back into Manhattan. It took me a little longer to reach the city because I avoided speeding with a gym bag containing 250,000 ecstasy pills on the backseat of my new black Acura RL. In addition to whatever business Vito Rizzuto had with Massino officially, Rizzuto also had opened a backchannel to the Bonanno family in the person of Vinny."

According to Dominick, "Vinny, in fact, made several trips to Canada with the goal of reopening the drug pipeline into New York. Vinny was truly a slickster, going to a doctor in Canada for his hair transplants. Vinny had used that as a cover to meet with Vito so the two Bonanno family members could reestablish the lucrative drug connection. The drugs were now flowing in on a biweekly basis. Vinny and Anthony 'Bruno' Indelicato were getting massive quantities of high-grade marijuana, along with ecstasy pills. They were both rocking and rolling in the drug trade, all without Big Joe even hearing a word of what was going on.

"The Bronx was different animal. It's like we were on a different planet altogether as far as Massino and the other crews in the family were concerned. With the pipeline in full force, Vinny's relationship with Vito became solid and Vito knew that Vinny could be trusted. Not to mention that Vito knew that Vinny and George had been extremely close friends. Now with the pipeline of drugs running smoothly on a biweekly basis, Vinny and Bruno were making some serious dough. But as fast as it came in, Vinny was gambling it all away. Vinny was flying on Learjets all over the country to gamble. The fact is, Vinny Gorgeous was the mirror image of John Gotti. The two mob bosses were degenerate gamblers. Vinny even got himself barred from Atlantic City. The gambler and the cokehead Bruno were actually spending more than they were reaping in drug profits. On the night Vinny paged me, it was as part of an effort to appease Vito in Montreal."

Cicale estimated that Vinny and Bruno owed more than $180,000 for marijuana, and around $375,000 for the 250,000 ecstasy pills. "The gym bag was still stuffed with ecstasy pills because apparently it was not a drug in demand among Vinny and Bruno's dealers at the time." Cicale said. "Vinny and Bruno didn't have a clue as to how to get rid of the pills."

With the delay in payment to Vito, the biweekly shipments stopped altogether. Finally after about two months of not receiving payment, Vinny sent word up to Vito, who in return sent some soldiers from Canada to New York to meet with Vinny alone.

"What the fuck am I doing," Dominick was thinking that night in July as he drove, carefully and legally, into Manhattan.

"I hadn't earned a penny off the drugs and if I was stopped now and my vehicle searched, I would be fucked, big time. I would go to jail for life—and just for doing a favor…"

As luck would have it that evening, I was never stopped and the drop-off of drugs went smoothly without a hitch. Around two weeks later, Cicale found himself meeting with what he termed "the Canadian transport team." Cicale handed them $25,000. This knocked down the bill from the family's Montreal crew. Vinny and Bruno were now waiting for the biweekly shipments to start up again so they could reap and spend more fortunes. However, fate outsmarted them when an elderly couple who'd been driving the drugs to New York was caught by law enforcement somewhere along their journey.

The drug pipeline from Canada was halted for good, as far as Cicale knows.

# 10   BAD TIMES FOR BONANNOS

In the film Goodfellas, Henry Hill eventually says: "These were the bad times."

Likewise, the bad times had arrived for the Bonanno family. Unable to penetrate Massino's operation via conventional investigative routes, the FBI got inventive, turning loose forensic accountants from financial fraud. In 2000, they hit pay dirt. A Manhattan parking lot magnate named Barry Weinberg was found to be the weak link in the long chain leading to those close to Massino. Raised in Sheepshead Bay, Brooklyn in a Jewish family, Weinberg had reaped a fortune in the parking lot business. A chatty chain smoker, Weinberg also was a sharp businessman who held a lifelong fascination for the Mafia. When Weinberg was able to partner with a wiseguy, he loved it, believing it would benefit him because he'd have more clout in his business dealings. Weinberg went on record with Bonanno capo Richard "Shellackhead" Cantarella, who first got involved in crime back in the late 1970s working with a Manhattan city councilman with whom he eventually earned hundreds of thousands of dollars from lease scams in the Staten Island Ferry terminals, among other things. Cantarella murdered the former councilman after he believed the man had become addicted to drugs, which would have left them both vulnerable.

Cantarella went on to extort wealthy businessmen. He had, in fact, once kidnapped a businessman and stole everything of value in his home. Cantarella then forced the same man to continue to pay him protection money. Cantarella was known to resort to violence whenever it helped to serve him, even in his legitimate businesses. When an underling supposedly complained about the level of violence, Cantarella said, "This is the Mafia— I don't care."

Shellackhead had his eyes focused on the family's top job. Cicale, who didn't know Cantarella very well, nevertheless related one revealing

37

anecdote about Shellackhead.

"He'd wear Boss-branded sweatshirts and in one encounter with Vinny Gorgeous, "Shellackhead" pointed to the brand's logo on his chest and said: That's gonna be me.""

When he met Weinberg, Cantarella leaped at the opportunity to enter the parking lot business—or rather steal as much money from it as humanly possible. The only problem was that Weinberg had left himself vulnerable to the Feds by not reporting millions of dollars of income he'd earned over the years. The FBI nabbed Weinberg and told him that they had enough evidence to put him in prison for the rest of his life. Or, he was told, he could wear a wire for the Feds and incriminate every Bonanno with whom he spoke. Weinberg—and one of his business associates—agreed to cooperate, eventually generating hundreds of incriminating discussions with Shellackhead, as well as various members of his crew. In October 2002, armed with this evidence, the government brought a 24-count RICO indictment against 21 Bonanno soldiers and associates. The biggest names on the indictment were Cantarella, who was acting underboss while Vitale was awaiting sentencing for loan sharking and money laundering, and capo Frank Coppa.

Vinny Gorgeous and Dominick Cicale were among the family members on the street wondering what was going on.

"Before we knew it the playing field in the Bonanno crime family was changing at a rapid pace. People were getting locked up left and right," said Cicale. "Most of the arrests were out of Queens, Brooklyn and Staten Island. The Feds finally, after more than 60 years of Mafia history, were able to break the code of silence within the Bonanno crime family. In 2002, a made man in the Bonanno family agreed to cooperate with the government. That man was Frankie Coppa."

Coppa would directly implicate Massino in the murder of Dominick "Sonny Black" Napolitano, and also implicated Cantarella and Vitale in the 1992 murder of a New York Post delivery superintendent who was a Bonanno associate. Not very long afterward, Cantarella also agreed to cooperate and testify against Massino and Vitale. Cicale, along with other members of the Bonanno family, found the defections particularly difficult to swallow.

"Out of the five New York City crime families, we were the only one that never had a made man rat," Cicale said. "We would puff our chests out to the other families, who by that time had many cooperators with the government. It felt great; no one could say shit about us. The only thing they could say was that in the early days we had an undercover cop infiltrate our organization. When Massino was finally arrested on January 9, 2003, we had Anthony "Tony Green" Urso running the show."

Urso's tenure proved to be short but memorable. Little is known of his early life, except that he was dyslexic. He moved to New York City and eventually hooked up with the Bonanno crime family. In the 1970s, Urso became a made man in the crew of Dominick "Sonny Black" Napolitano. Following Napolitano's 1983 murder, Urso was placed in Massino's crew. Eventually, he grew close to Massino and drove for him. By 1988, it is believed that Urso was elevated to capo. In the 1990s, then-underboss Vitale grew increasingly jealous of Urso's new power in the family and attempted to persuade Massino to murder Urso based on fabricated accusations.

"Vitale was my biggest enemy within the family, so much so that on several occasions he attempted to have me killed by bringing false accusations against me," Urso later stated in a letter prior to his sentencing. "These accusations were dismissed as ridiculous by Massino because he knew of the jealousy on Vitale's part, and Massino knew that I was a loyal friend to him."

Urso commanded the Bonanno family and had major resources to back him up.

Anthony 'Tony Green' Urso was also interested in attractive young ladies—to a fault. On street corner meetings, he was known to suddenly lose interest in the topic of discussion whenever a fetching young woman happened into his field of vision. "Tony thought he was God's gift to every woman who passed him by," Cicale said. "He'd make it so obvious too, looking a woman up and down."

"Urso was single and in his late 60s-early 70s. He looked good for his age," Cicale said. "Tony Green stood about 5-foot-8 and weighed around 170 pounds and was always hanging out at the gym, the tanning bed, and nightclubs." Cicale recalled a time when he and Basciano were waiting for Urso to meet them. "Urso steps out of his tricked-out, pimped-out black Hummer H2 wearing bright, shiny, royal-blue skintight spandex. Urso actually looked as if he was about to get on stage at a male strip club.

"Vinny and I were standing in a supermarket parking lot waiting for Urso. We watched him park his car farther down the lot from us. When Urso got out of the Hummer in that outfit, Vinny starts whispering shit to me without moving his lips so Urso doesn't notice. 'Oh my fucking God,' Basciano told me. 'Is this man crazy or what? Dom, look at his sagging balls. They're huge. This guy is fucking kidding, right?'"

Smiling at the recollection, Cicale said, "Tony was only several feet away and I'm trying to hold in a major burst of laughter. I'm trying to keep my lips together and stop myself from losing it. Then Vinny whispered again, like a ventriloquist: 'Bo, shut the fuck up. You're gonna make me bust out laughing right in this guy's face. You're gonna get us killed.' I'm busting a gut inside, thinking if any of the other families see this guy, then we're all gonna get killed, the whole fucking crime family."

Urso walked towards them, arms outspread to give both Vinny and Dominick the standard wiseguy greeting with a kiss on each cheek. Basciano's whispered commentary still rang loudly in Dominick's head and Dominick was having great difficulty maintaining his composure. As Vinny and Urso hugged, Dominick suddenly leaned over.

"A loud sound had come out of my mouth," Dominick said. "I acted like I was gagging to cover up my laughter. I knew at that moment that Vinny wanted to kill me. Finally, after what seemed like forever, I straightened back up with tears rolling down my cheeks. I kept acting like I was choking."

Dominick, pretending that he had something stuck in his throat, walked back to his car to get a drink as Vinny had thoughtfully suggested. As he was halfway to the car, Tony started calling out to Dom, with true concern in his voice: "Dom! You sure you're okay! You need help?" Dominick raised his hand, indicating that he was okay and didn't require the Heimlich maneuver, which Urso appeared ready to apply.

"Once in the car I turned on the engine, placing my head against the steering wheel. I started laughing so hard that I almost pissed myself. It took me at least five minutes to compose myself."

In addition to the skintight spandex, Urso wore a toupee—which was crooked. "It was half-on and half-off his head," Cicale said. "Not to mention, Tony was so overly tanned from the hours on tanning beds that his scalp, which was normally covered by the hairpiece, was exposed and was a totally different color than the rest of him."

Dominick had finally composed himself enough to return to Urso, the acting boss of the Bonanno family, and Vinny.

I knew Vinny's every move and if I hadn't caused such a scene, Vinny would have told Tony to fix his toupee. But Vinny knew if he did that now or anytime during the conversation, Tony would realize that my coughing fit was not a coughing fit at all. So Vinny was now forced to keep his mouth shut, and we were both forced to continue to look at this spectacle."

Once the discussion had ended, Vinny and Dominick were back inside their car watching Anthony "Tony Green" Urso drive away in his humongous vehicle. They could finally break into uproarious laughter getting it all out of their system.

"Five minutes later, we were finally pulling out of the supermarket parking lot heading back into the Bronx. Vinny told me that I could never do that again and that I had to control myself. As Vinny said that, I quickly turned my attention from the road to him. Just by my look, he knew that I was thinking: 'Okay Bo, but this was no doubt a huge exception...'"

And they both burst into another round of laughter. Dominick said that Tony Green may have had the title, but it was Vinny Basciano who was pulling the strings from the background. One evening during Urso's brief run as acting boss, Dominick was hanging out at the nightclub Rain, located in the lavish Garden City Hotel on Long Island. Accompanying him were Anthony "Ace" Aiello and an Irish friend of Cicale's named Jimmy. "Tony Green" was there as well, but this time dressed in appropriate attire, his hairpiece properly adjusted.

"Actually he was a good looking guy," Cicale said. "He was all tanned up and wearing jeans and a tight shirt that showed off his physique." Dominick, Ace and Jimmy approached Urso, who was with a few guys. Introductions went all around. "Tony pulls me to the side and asks me if my friend Jimmy is a cop. I look at him thinking: Are you kidding me? I am a Bonanno crime family captain. And you have the fucking balls to ask me if I am hanging out with a cop. I keep my composure and tell him, 'No, Tony, Jimmy is not a cop, he is a very dear friend of mine who I met in federal prison.'"

Okay, said Tony, adding that he was "just curious." Then, Tony pointed at one of the guys he had introduced to Dominick. He and the others had their backs to Tony and Dominick. "That guy John I just introduced you to... he is a cop," Tony told a disbelieving Dominick.

"Okay," Dominick said, feeling like he had fallen through the rabbit hole and was in Wonderland. An acting boss of a Mafia family hanging out with a cop and introducing him to his guys? To Dominick, this was simply too much to digest so he promptly reported the matter to Basciano the next day.

"Vinny could not believe what I had told him. He had me repeat it to him—several times—so he could fully absorb the actions of the man who was the acting boss of the family. At the end of the day, Vinny felt it best to remain silent and continue pulling the strings from behind the scenes. Yep, Tony Green was Vinny's puppet."

Vincent "Vinny Gorgeous" Basciano was—and remains—truly in control of the Bonanno crime family. "We were the power in the Bonanno crime family," said Dominick, adding, "I was Vinny's right hand. He could count on me for anything."

Everything was running smoothly until another arrest came down. Anthony "Tony Green" Urso, who Dominick would come to refer to as "Stripper Man," was taken into custody. In 2004, as a result of several meetings with wired informant, Bonanno capo James "Big Lou" Tartaglione, Urso was indicted on racketeering, murder, gambling, loansharking and extortion charges.

Urso was caught on Big Lou's tape famously proclaiming what he believed should be new mob policy as regards turncoats: "Why should the rats' kids be happy, where my kids or your kids should suffer because I'm away for life?" Urso asked. "If you take one kid, I hate to say it, and do what you gotta do, the [rats] will fucking think twice."

In February 2005, Urso pleaded guilty to all charges and was sentenced to 17 years in a federal prison. Urso's projected release date is December 5, 2021.

Vinny Gorgeous no longer had Urso for cover, but now he was officially in charge. He assumed control of the Bonanno crime family as its acting boss. Massino, from his prison cell, concurred and let Vinny know he had the power. Moreover, it was common knowledge that Dominick Cicale was Vinny's second in command, even though Dominick was not officially part of the official administration.

# 11  WASHERWOMEN

As the new acting boss, Vinny immediately started making changes, said Cicale.

Rank and hierarchy are concepts used flexibly in the mob. The Genovese family used "front bosses" to shield their real boss ever since Vito Genovese died and Benny Squint Lombardo assumed control.

In the Gambino family, according to former undercover FBI agent Joaquin "Jack Falcone" Garcia, Gambino boss Arnold "Zeke" Squitieri had not appointed a panel, but rather had arranged for a capo and soldier close to him to run the day-to-day operations. Acting underboss Anthony Megale was involved with overseeing rackets in the Stamford, Connecticut area, while Squitieri's main man on the street was his nephew, Louis Filippelli, who officially held the rank of soldier under Gambino capo Alphonse "Funzi" Sisca. Sisca himself was Squitieri's brother-in-law. So owing to Funzi's higher rank, Zeke made it known that Sisca had the power, but unofficially, Filippelli was Zeke's eyes and ears. Also, Chris Sucarato was only an associate in Funzi's crew at the time, but due to his close ties to both Filippelli and Funzi, he had more power than most associates.

Likewise, in the Bonanno family, Basciano and Cicale held the power. Vinny elevated Michael "Mikey Nose" Mancuso to acting underboss; Anthony "Mr. Fish" Rabito was named acting consigliere; and Nicky "Mouth" Santoro became an official captain. In addition, Sal "The Iron Worker" Montagna became an acting capo, taking control of Patrick "Patty from the Bronx" DeFilippo's Bronx crew. (Patty had been incarcerated).

"First order of business for me was to go out for a few drinks with Sal and some guys," said Dominick. "It was a Thursday evening around nine when we all gathered together at a place in Manhattan called Merchants."

The well-appointed Merchants NY Cigar Bar is one of the few such places in Manhattan that are licensed for cigar smoking. According to its website, its design includes a rich carpet and plush furniture with hints of an English Gentlemen's Club. Its Victorian influences give a sense of elegance and luxury of a bygone era. A marble-topped bar and a year-round fireplace provide a warm, relaxed setting that beckons guests to savor their favorite drinks with friends and associates whilst enjoying the best cigars.

Dominick held court at Merchants as often as he could, enjoying a Cohiba Robusto or Romeo & Julieta Numero Dos, while sipping a single-malt scotch, bourbon, cognac, port or grappa, depending on his mood. That evening, Sal "The Iron Worker" arrived with Little Patty, another made man in the Bonanno crime family.

"Patty stood just over 5-foot and had the build of a fireplug," Cicale said.

Dominick, who was inducted in the same ceremony with Little Patty, said, "I liked Little Patty a lot. He had served an 18-year stint in prison and was in Fat Patty's Bronx-based crew that was by then overseen by Sal 'The Iron' Worker."

Dominick had arrived with Anthony "Ace" Aiello from Queens and Nicholas "PJ" Pisciotti from New Jersey. PJ was Cicale's acting capo and Ace was a soldier in Cicale's Bronx-based crew, which had formerly been Basciano's crew.

"I called Ace, my 'Ace Boom Coon' and sometimes 'Luca Brasi.'"

Sal "The Iron Worker" also hung out in Ridgewood, Queens where there were lots of Zips. He loved the social clubs. In fact, Sal and Ace's cousin, Giuseppe "Joey" Gambina, would hang in the same clubs, drinking and playing cards. Joey was a Zip as well.

"Joey Gambina was only an associate but was around me," said Dominick. "The only reason why he was not there that evening was the fact that he was not a made man yet. Joey was considered an underdog, but I loved the underdogs and I knew I could polish Joey up. From there, the sky was the limit for him."

Joey was known for his hard drinking and drug use, mainly sniffing cocaine. In the Mafia, this is severely frowned upon. Selling drugs (as long as you don't get caught) is one thing, but doing drugs is considered taboo—an obvious case of the mob's hypocrisy in Dominick's view.

"I hated the fact that most of these dick suckers wanna be tough guys and talk like they never once did a drug or sucked a cunt. (Cunnilingus is an even darker taboo than doing drugs; it is considered "sucking dick by proxy.") C'mon, are you kidding me? Don't get me wrong. I know we can't be high because it can affect how we act and what we say; we always have to maintain our composure on the street. But to knock someone for partying as a young man is outrageous. I know men who are in high positions in the Mafia right now, even a boss of one of the five families who used both cocaine and heroin as a teenager."

That night in Merchants, the group was hanging around having drinks. Based upon their rank as capos, Dominick and Sal sat next to each other while the rest sat around them.

"It was a respect thing and showed to everyone who was in control," Cicale said. "All the men in my crew were well-schooled in the traditions of mob life. If anyone came into that restaurant and went to shake the hand of one of my men before my hand, my man would refuse and direct that person to me. They would say, 'Go shake Dominick's hand first.'"

During the course of the evening, Sal leaned in close to Dominick and asked if he could have a word alone with him. "Of course I would listen to what Sal had to say," said Dominick. "I excused us both from the group so we could talk in private. I know some made men who would've ordered everyone off the table to showboat, but that wasn't my style. Those Mafiosi who go too far with ordering their men around are basically suffering from insecurity."

Sal explained to Dominick that Ace's cousin, Joey Gambina, and another Zip, also a Bonanno associate, had been in an argument while playing cards and having drinks in a social club. The Iron Worker himself wasn't present to witness the event, but apparently he'd been informed. Sal told Dominick that Joey was in the wrong—and that since Joey was around Dominick, it was a reflection on Dominick—and thus his problem. What likely fueled Montagna's complaint was the fact that Joey was considered a cokehead in the mob because of his heavy partying.

"I listened to Sal's story. To me it was all bullshit but I had to still listen and make a show that I was truly concerned. So I sat silently for an hour listening to Sal talk."

After Sal was finished with his "washwoman bullshit" as Dominick refers to it, Dominick then replied to Sal, telling him, "Sal, you're my dear friend. There are three sides to every story; Joey's, your guy's, and the truth. Listen, neither one of us was there when the argument happened. Why don't we bring them both together and see if they can resolve the matter in our presence?" Sal agreed with Dominick.

"That was it. We went back to the group and enjoyed the rest of the evening. At that time, I was seeing Vinny every day. We were pretty much inseparable. Two days after the gathering, Vinny asked me about my conversation with Sal. I looked at him with a questioning expression and said, 'Nothing. Why?'"

Vinny asked Dominick twice, and when Dominick held to his position, Vinny told him that Sal had relayed an entirely different version of the story to Mancuso. "According to Sal, when we are all together that evening at Merchant's, I had basically told him to go fuck himself," Dominick said. "Sal added that I had said that Joey can do whatever the fuck he wants and that if anyone has anything to say about it, I will deal with them. Mancuso also told Vinny that Sal had remained silent because he was well aware that I, in addition to being a captain, had Basciano's ear."

Dominick, upon hearing of Sal's story, flipped out. He called Sal a "motherfucking liar." He also told Vinny that he was immediately driving to Queens, where Sal was known to hang out in the Ridgewood-area social clubs where the family's Zips tended to socialize.

"Vinny was trying to calm me but I was not having it, so it was my own fault what happened next. There was another Bonanno family acting captain with us and Vinny wasn't going to take any shit from me in front of him. So Vinny ripped me a new asshole, telling me that I wasn't going to do a fucking thing and that he was the boss. Vinny was pretty pissed, and when he flipped out on me, I had enough sense to finally shut the fuck up and take it. I knew I had disrespected a man who I held in the highest respect and that I was in the wrong. I gave Vinny no choice that night and had to take my lumps, especially with another captain there watching how Vinny held himself."

Despite Vinny's outburst at Dominick, Vinny did investigate Sal's complaint further. "It took Vinny a matter of hours to get to the bottom of it. In the end, it was the fault of Mikey Nose, the biggest washwoman of them all. Mikey admitted to Vinny that he maybe embellished the story a little. Then it was Mikey Nose's turn to face Basciano's wrath.

"Vinny told Michael that if he ever did anything like that again, Vinny would not think twice about stripping him down to the rank of a soldier."

When Vinny informed Dominick about Mancuso's role in the story, Dominick disliked Mancuso even more than he had previously. "I never liked Michael," Dominick said. "I abused him, even before I was a made man. I was an associate and Michael dogged it when I called him out. As for Sal, I knew that he also had done his own embellishing. I knew from then on that I'd have to watch my words very carefully around Sal."

Sal, however, wouldn't prove to be a problem for Cicale. His relationship with Mancuso further deteriorated. A murder plot would first be put into motion.

# 12  NO ONE EVER WALKS AWAY PEACEFULLY

A year passed with Vinny as boss of the Bonanno crime family. He and Dominick routinely met for hours every day, always at different times and places.

Christmas was approaching—the time of gift-giving—the most popular holiday for Cosa Nostra bosses.

The previous Christmas, while "Tony Green" was on the streets, Vito Rizzuto sent $25,000 down from Canada.

"Vito was part of the Bonannos and he did as every other captain did during the holiday—he gave money to the boss of the crime family as a show of appreciation," Cicale noted. "For this upcoming Christmas, Vinny sent word with Sal that Vito had to step it up and send $100,000. So Vito sent the money."

With Vinny arrested in November 2014, he would not be on the street when the tribute arrived. Dominick, however, was still a major player in the Bonanno family. Dominick was Vinny's eyes and ears on the street, which didn't sit well with Vinny's appointed acting boss, Michael Mancuso.

"I found myself running things with Mancuso," Dominick said. "This jerk-off actually challenged me as if I was a punk. Mr. Nose was in for a rude awaking."

Dominick was told by Vinny to act as Mancuso's unofficial enforcer, the same role he'd played for Basciano.

"I was now Michael's muscle," Dominick said. "My job was to back him all the way."

In no time, Mancuso "puffed his chest out," Dominick noted. Michael slapped around low-level associates in the streets of the Bronx for no good reason that Cicale could see.

"It was getting so out of hand that I told Michael to calm down a bit. But I could immediately see that he was offended. That was just the beginning. Messages were coming to me—orders to be relayed to Michael instructing him to do certain things. Michael, rather than just listening to me, wanted to know how I was getting the information, which was none of his concern."

Vinny had previously told Dominick that he should never explain to Mancuso how the orders were being relayed to him. Vinny expressly forbade this, trusting Dominick more than Mancuso—and actually putting Dominick in the middle as a buffer in case Mancuso flipped, which was not inconceivable considering all the recent Bonanno turncoats.

"So now Michael is testing the waters with me, seeing how far he could take it. But to his complete surprise, I put him in check on day one." Here is Dominick's reconstruction of the conversation:

MICHAEL: Hey Dom, you need to tell me everything. I am running the family here. I am not going to follow these instructions you are supposedly getting until you explain to me how these messages are coming to you.

DOM: Michael, please. I was instructed that by no means should I explain to you how I get the orders. This is what Joe and Vinny want to happen.

MICHAEL: Fuck that. I am not accepting any messages from you!

DOM: Please, Michael! We need to work together here. Vinny had plenty of conversations about how we were supposed to handle this if he was arrested. We're supposed to stick together and carry out Vinny's orders.

MICHAEL: How do I know you're not bullshitting me?

DOM: I don't need this crap! I am here for Vinny and only Vinny!

MICHAEL: Lower your voice when you talk to me!

DOM: Who the fuck do you think you are talking to? You are well aware that I am part of the controlling administration. If you have a problem with me, Michael, we can settle it now. By no means am I going to have you disrespect me. I'm not one of those street punks impressed with you. I know your history! Now whatever you want to do, let me know and let's do it!

MICHAEL: Dom, what the fuck! Why are you getting all crazy?

DOM: Because you are talking to me like I'm a jerk-off. I have been extremely patient and you keep on disrespecting me. I am not some stranger coming to you out of left field with these orders. So let's start over, before you force me to weaken your position as acting boss.

MICHAEL: Okay. Let's meet tomorrow, but I want to start changing the meet locations.

DOM: Whatever. That's fine by me. See you tomorrow. And please, don't try me again.

The next meeting didn't go so well, either, as Dominick related. "I held my composure, but Michael was still not accepting the orders that I was passing on to him. It really made no sense, but what choice did I have? I was not going to go against the wishes of the bosses because of Michael Nose's power trip. When Michael broke down the new locations for the meetings, I agreed. But I also noticed that all the places he'd chosen for future meetings were desolate areas. Michael was never going to trap me like that, so I just played the game and agreed. I was receiving word almost daily from Vinny, who was in jail with Joe Massino. I was also sending messages back to Vinny about Michael not accepting the messages. That is when I was told that if Michael didn't act on the orders, then it was my job to act on them."

Vinny was basically telling Dominick that if Mancuso didn't start taking orders, then Dominick was to usurp him. "That was something I was looking forward to," Dominick said. "The first message I acted on was to promote Louie Electric from acting capo to official capo. But first, I went to Michael to give him one last chance to accept Vinny's orders."

Louie drove Dominick to the meeting with Michael, who was already there waiting for Dominick. Louie waited in the car while Dominick got out and walked over to Mancuso.

DOM: Hey, what's going on?

MICHAEL: Nothing, Dom. What about you? Why is Louie sitting in the car?

DOM: I was instructed to pass this message along to you and if you choose not to accept it or act on it, then I am to take charge and act on the behalf of Joe, Vinny, and this crime family. Word came down that changes are to be made and the first one is that Louie will be promoted to official capo. Now, are you going to accept this and carry it out?

MICHAEL: Dominick, how are you getting these fucking messages!

DOM: Okay, Michael. You mean to tell me that once I let you know how these messages are getting passed to me, then you will accept them and act upon them?

MICHAEL: Yes, Dom! I will!

DOM: Then you can go fuck yourself. It's on you.

Dominick called out to Louie and held his hand up, waving Louie to join the two of them. Once he was there, Dominick told him: "Louie, I received word from Vinny that Joe agrees that you should be elevated from acting capo to official capo. Michael chose not act on this order, so I am telling you, as instructed. You are now an official capo in this crime family. Congratulations! Michael, I want you to meet Louie, who is now an official capo.

MICHAEL: Congratulations, Louie.

LOUIE: Thank you, Michael!

DOM: Louie, if you don't mind, can you give me and Michael a moment?

LOUIE: Sure Dom! Michael! Good seeing you!

MICHAEL: Same here Louie! And again, congratulations!

DOM: Do you realize what you just did? Michael, there are going to be other changes as well, and I don't need this bullshit. I don't want the fucking top spot! I wanna just do my own thing and make money. Will you just listen to these messages and follow them?

MICHAEL: Yeah, but first you need to tell me how these messages are coming to you.

DOM: I have to run. I'll catch up with you in a few days.

Dominick was in the middle now, moving men in and out of certain crews, collecting money for Vinny and Joe. Dominick met with official capos and the acting consiglieri. Everything was running smoothly and Mikey Nose was out of the picture—or so Dominick thought.

"Michael was doing things behind everyone's back and was splitting the crime family—or trying to. Finally I received the green light to punch Michael Nose's ticket. Everything was set to go in the beginning of February 2005. Michael would vanish off the face of the earth. No one would ever find the body of Michael "Mikey Nose" Mancuso. However, thanks to our wonderful federal government, "The Nose" was saved. I was arrested on January 27, 2005. God must have been watching over Michael Nose."

While in the Brooklyn lockup, Cicale was placed with Baldo Amato, one of the family's Zips. "Baldo was facing a life sentence and was still doing time for past crimes," Dominick said. "Baldo was close with Sal 'The Iron Worker.' They had hung out together in Ridgewood at the social clubs. Another year had almost passed and Christmas was once again around the corner. But this time I was jailed along with Vinny. Baldo had just received word from the street that the year when Sal went to Canada to retrieve the $100,000, Vito was extremely upset. They gave Sal shit, but in the end they still paid up. Vinny had the power now (he was named the Bonanno crime family official boss after news was released that Massino was cooperating with the federal government). Actually, Joe ultimately is the reason that Vinny and I were arrested. With Vinny now calling the shots from his prison cell, Vinny made sure that Michael "Mikey Nose" Mancuso was in full charge on the street. Vinny knew that keeping the power with someone he could fully control was important, and Michael was the perfect puppet."

However, not long afterwards, Mancuso also was arrested. Vinny then put Sal "The Iron Worker" in charge as acting boss. "Vinny knew Sal was another puppet he could control," Cicale said.

But word reached Dominick that the family's old timers did not want Sal in the acting boss slot. They called him the "Bambino Boss" because he was so young and was viewed as lacking the appropriate experience. "Even Montagna himself was aware of this and started carrying a weapon," Dominick said.

The government was relentless. They ended up deporting Sal back to Canada. The government did not want Vinny to have any control from prison whatsoever. But when Sal was deported and tried to run things in Canada, he lost focus on his surroundings. He found himself in a no-win situation—a trap. Sal was found shot to death by the Royal Mounted Canadian Police.

"Last I'd heard was that Sal was entangled in a bullshit turf war," said Dominick. "That's the way it goes in the Mafia. It's life in prison or you get whacked or you become a rat.

"No one ever walks away peacefully.

# BIBLIOGRAPHY

**The Sixth Family: The Collapse of the New York Mafia and the Rise of Vito Rizzuto** by Adrian Humphreys and Lee Lamothe.

**The Enforcer: Johnny Pops Papalia: A Life and Death in the Mafia** by Adrian Humphreys.

**The Mob and the City: The Hidden History of How the Mafia Captured New York** by Alex Hortis.

**Five Families: The Rise, Decline, and Resurgence of America's Most Powerful Mafia Empires** by Selwyn Raab

**King of the Godfathers: Joseph Massino and the Fall of the Bonanno Crime Family** by Anthony DeStefano

**Vinny Gorgeous: The Ugly Rise And Fall Of A New York Mobster** by Anthony DeStefano

**Last Days of the Sicilians: At War with the Mafia** by Ralph Blumenthal

**The Pizza Connection: Lawyers, Money, Drugs, Mafia** by Shana Alexander

**The Last Godfather: The Rise and Fall of Joey Massino** by Simon Crittle

**Bringing Down the Mob: The War Against the American Mafia** by Thomas Reppetto

**Nothing But Money: How the Mob Infiltrated Wall Street** by Greg B. Smith

**Mob Testimony: Joe Pistone, Michael Scars DiLeonardo, Angelo Lonardo and others** by Richard Willoughby

**Mafia Inc.: The Long, Bloody Reign of Canada's Sicilian Clan** by Andre Cedilot and Andre Noel

**Newspaper article:**

The New York Times:

Joe Bonanno Dies; Mafia Leader, 97, Who Built Empire by SELWYN RAAB, published: May 12, 2002

CosaNostraNews.com

# ABOUT THE AUTHORS

Ed Scarpo is the pseudonym of a New York-based journalist who has reported on everything from venture capital finance to the entertainment industry. For years he's also been reporting on the Mafia for his Cosa Nostra News blog. Scarpo has interviewed and written about many former gangsters, as well as lawmen and true-crime authors. The Cicale Files, Volume One: Inside the Last Great Mafia Empire is his first book.

Dominick Cicale, a feared capo in the Bonanno crime family, was privy to the inner workings of organized crime and was a rising star in New York's Mafia until family boss Joseph Massino was arrested and then turned on his own people. Massino's betrayal took down Cicale, his mentor, "Vinny Gorgeous" Basciano, and others. Facing pressure from his Mafia cohorts to offer false testimony, Cicale cooperated with federal authorities and has testified in four major RICO trials.

**COMING SOON:**
**Cicale Files, Volume Two:**
**Nothing Personal**

Made in the USA
Lexington, KY
31 August 2015